A QUINTET BOOK

ISBN: 0-7858-0339-4

This book was designed and produced by
Quintet Publishing Limited
6, Blundell Street
London N7 9BH

Art Director: Peter Bridgewater
Editor: Suzanne Luchford
Jacket Design: Nik Morley

Typeset in Great Britain by
Central Southern Typesetters, Eastbourne
Manufactured in China by
Regent Publishing Services Limited.

This edition produced for sale in the USA,
its territories and dependencies only.

Published by Chartwell Books
A Division of Book Sales, Inc.
P.O. Box 7100
Edison, New Jersey 08818–7100

Contents

Setting the Scene

The Bible makes vast claims for itself. It tells its readers that they can find the secrets of the universe within its pages, the whole pattern of history from the very beginning to the present day.

It opens with a picture of absolute, irresistible power. In six brief passages covering six days, it depicts the creation of the whole universe, and everything it contains, made to one single plan with mankind at its centre. It continues with explanations of the origins of evil, war, the struggle to earn a living, and the divisions between races and nations.

The opening chapters of the Book of Genesis are far more than descriptions of people, events and places. For Jewish and Christian believers they tell of God as he uses his cosmic powers to save mankind. Throughout the Bible God is playwright, director and actor in the drama of salvation, whose presence can be detected in everything that happens.

At the time when the Bible was first written, its readers were familiar with the events described, for they took place largely in their own times and their own country. In order to appreciate these writings today we need to discover all we can about the places where biblical events took place, and about the people who were involved in them.

Genesis

Genesis was written as an introduction to the main event in Hebrew history, the exodus, when the ancestors of the Hebrews made their escape from slavery in Egypt under the leadership of Moses. The escape itself and its immediate consequences are described in the books of Exodus, Leviticus, Numbers and Deuteronomy. The whole account was finally edited towards the end of the Old Testament period.

The final editors of these opening books of the Bible looked back over nearly 2,000 years of Hebrew history and saw how it had been shaped by its beginnings. The traditions which Jesus inherited as a Jew were deeply influenced by the exodus from Egypt, 13 centuries earlier, and by the stories of

ABOVE *Landscape with cranes. The creation is described as an ordered perfect whole in which everything – and everyone has its place.*

Abraham and his descendants four centuries before this. Genesis sets the scene for the whole Hebrew tradition and explains the forces at work in it.

An Ordered World

There are two accounts of the creation of the universe in Genesis. The first describes an ordered world with mankind as its administrator, where everything is part of one perfect plan. The second account is more primitive and personal as it explains the origins of sexual desire and sets the scene for the emergence of evil and enmity.

Hebrew author of Genesis as he scraped a living in the harsh conditions of Palestine, for the Mesopotamian rivers Tigris and Euphrates are two of the four rivers which watered the Garden of Eden.

The great floods of Mesopotamia were models and reminders of the first, universal flood. When the waters subsided, Noah's ark grounded on the mountains of the Ararat range, north of Mesopotamia near the head-waters of the river Tigris.

Ancestors

The nomadic shepherd ancestor of all Hebrews, Abraham, entered Canaan (the earlier name for Palestine) about 1800 BC as he and his family moved their flocks along the traditional grazing routes between Mesopotamia and Egypt. The covenants God made with Abraham are enormously impor-tant, even today, for they are the basis of Hebrew claims to Palestine, 'The Holy Land', stretching from the Egyptian border to Syria, and from the Mediterranean coast to the eastern edge of the Jordan valley and the Dead Sea.

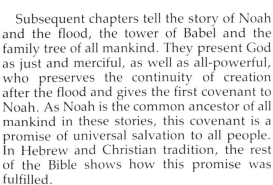

Subsequent chapters tell the story of Noah and the flood, the tower of Babel and the family tree of all mankind. They present God as just and merciful, as well as all-powerful, who preserves the continuity of creation after the flood and gives the first covenant to Noah. As Noah is the common ancestor of all mankind in these stories, this covenant is a promise of universal salvation to all people. In Hebrew and Christian tradition, the rest of the Bible shows how this promise was fulfilled.

The opening chapters of the Book of Genesis are set in Mesopotamia, the wide, fertile land of great rivers east of Palestine, beyond the deserts of Syria and Arabia. Mesopotamia seemed a paradise to the

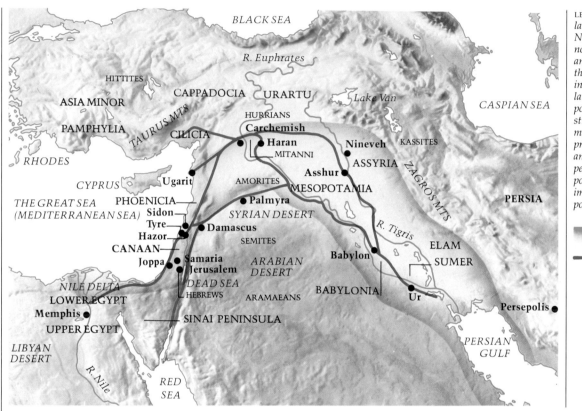

LEFT The great arc of fertile land stretching from the Nile delta in Lower Egypt north through Palestine and then south and east to the Persian Gulf. The intrinsic fertility of the land in Palestine and its position on the narrowest strip of the fertile crescent meant that it was highly prized by both nomadic and settled agricultural peoples and made it a point of strategic importance to the local powers.

'Fertile crescent'

Major trade routes

The stories about Abraham and his immediate descendants also connect the Hebrews with ancient Canaanite sanctuaries, which later became centres of the Hebrew religion. Even Jerusalem is mentioned, under its Canaanite name Salem, when its king brought gifts to Abraham. The city did not become the Hebrew capital until David captured it 800 years later.

The Canaanites were farmers who worked the fertile agricultural lands near their fortified settlements, while the Hebrew shepherds kept to the sparse grazing areas away from the 'cities'. Consequently, there was no direct competition between the nomadic Hebrews and the Canaanites at this time.

The Migration to Egypt

Egypt exercised a loose control over the region, particularly after 1640 BC when northern Egypt was captured by foreign rulers, the Hyksos, who were distantly related to the Hebrews. The Hyksos kings ruled

from Tanis and Avaris in the delta region of Egypt where the River Nile fans out into many channels as it enters the sea. Native Egyptians retained control of Upper Egypt south of the delta, which they ruled from Thebes.

This is the setting for the final chapters of Genesis, which describe the migation of the Hebrew shepherds to Egypt during a general famine. The main Hebrew figure is Joseph, who had been sold into slavery by his brothers and taken to Egypt, where he prospered and married the daughter of the high priest of the city of On (Heliopolis).

On, situated between Tanis and Avaris, was an important centre. The high priest of On bore the title 'Greatest of the Seers' and 'King's Son of his Body'. As a seer himself and the high priest's son-in-law, Joseph gained high rank in the Egyptian royal court where he could ensure that his Hebrew brethren would be welcome in Egypt.

The Hebrews settled in Goshen in the eastern part of the Nile delta, where they could escape the prolonged drought in their traditional grazing areas. But their fortunes would change when the native Egyptians dislodged (displaced) the Hyksos rulers a century later.

The Egyptians

There is virtually no rainfall in Egypt itself. The River Nile draws its waters from the highlands of Ethiopia and the tropical rain forests of central Africa. Consequently, Egypt could produce dependable crops, even when

ABOVE *Irrigation transforms arid desert into a garden; virtually the whole of Egypt's agricultural system depended on the waters of the River Nile.*

LEFT *The River Euphrates, one of the great rivers of the ancient world. Exploitation of the Euphrates in Mesopotamia for irrigation when the Hebrews arrived there was further advanced than it is today.*

the whole of the eastern Mediterranean region was struck by drought. This was achieved by controlling the Nile's summer floods and by using irrigation channels to water the crops when the river level fell again in the autumn.

Egyptian rulers always found it difficult to maintain control over the whole country because of the contrast between the broad lands of the delta where the Nile entered the sea, and the narrow ribbon of fertile land, 600 miles (1000 km) long, either side of the river from the First Cataract to the delta. In the shifting patterns of Egyptian politics, power moved between Lower Egypt (the delta region) and Upper Egypt, between Memphis and Thebes, as different groups gained control and founded dynasties.

Divine Kings

The Egyptian king (the pharaoh) was himself a god and the earthly representative of the gods, but his authority was constantly undermined by the rich and powerful priesthood, even though the priests served the gods as representatives of the king. The country was administered by a highly organized bureaucracy manned by priests. The king's real power rested with the army which was an efficient, mobile force organized in units of 250 foot soldiers supported by light chariots.

Each administrative district had its own court of law, presided over by an official of the central government. As Egypt was ruled by a divine dictator there was no central code of law, but records were kept and decisions were influenced by precedents.

Egyptian religion regulated every aspect of the people's lives and subsequent death. Egyptian tombs were lavishly furnished with all that the dead would need during their journey through the underworld towards judgement: tools, furniture, weapons and food, and even houses, either real or as clay models. Some of the royal tombs, the pyramids, were already 15 centuries old when Abraham entered Egypt.

The country grew a wide range of crops: wheat for bread, barley for beer, cattle fodder, dates, citrus fruit, and vegetables for eating and for oil. Flax was cultivated for Egypt's famous linen, and the papyrus reed for paper.

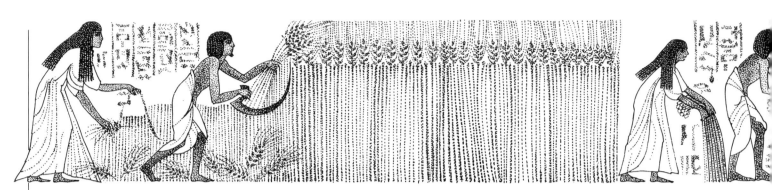

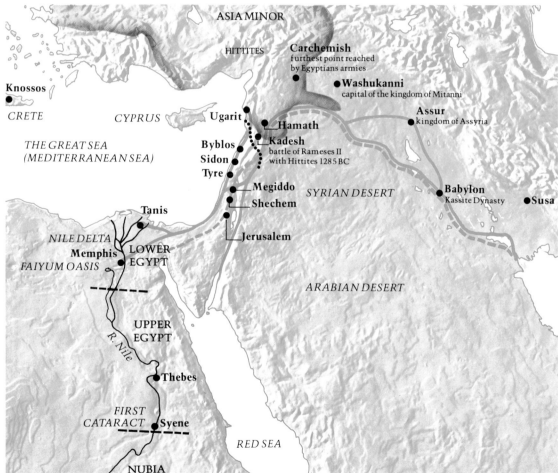

RIGHT *Egypt's prosperity depended as much on internal stability as it did on the wider regional balance of power. The strong Hittite kingdom to the north in Asia Minor and that of the Mittani in north west Mesopotamia limited Egyptian expansion even during times of relative domestic peace.*

--- *Pasturage routes of Hebrew nomads*

••••••• *Egyptian frontier under Rameses II in Syria*

Hittite empire

Major trade routes

– – – *Frontiers*

ASIA MINOR

HITTITES

Carchemish
furthest point reached by Egyptians armies

●**Washukanni**
capital of the kingdom of Mitanni

Knossos

Assur
kingdom of Assyria

CRETE

CYPRUS

Ugarit

*THE GREAT SEA
(MEDITERRANEAN SEA)*

Hamath

Byblos   **Kadesh**
                    battle of Rameses II
Sidon   with Hittites 1285 BC

Tyre

Babylon
Kassite Dynasty

●**Susa**

Megiddo

SYRIAN DESERT

Shechem

Tanis

Jerusalem

NILE DELTA

Memphis   LOWER
              EGYPT
FAIYUM OASIS

ARABIAN DESERT

**UPPER
EGYPT**

R. Nile

Thebes

*FIRST
CATARACT* **Syene**

RED SEA

NUBIA

Bundles of papyrus were lashed together and used to build boats for sailing the Nile, with their characteristic raised bows and sterns; they were often large enough for ocean voyages.

Slavery and Freedom

Fortunes changed dramatically for the Hebrew shepherds in Egypt when the foreign Hyksos kings were overthrown by native Egyptians. The Hebrews found themselves drafted into labour gangs to build frontier fortifications for the new dynasty. As the adopted child of an Egyptian princess, the Hebrew Moses might have been able to help but he had to flee Egypt after killing an overseer of Hebrew slaves.

Moses returned from his desert exile con-

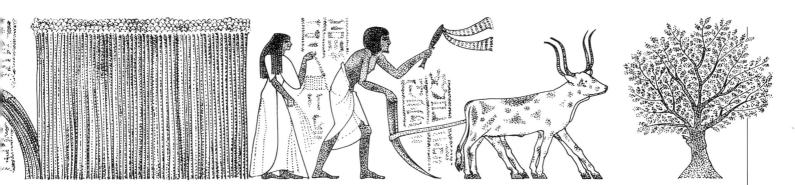

ABOVE *A frieze showing a harvest in ancient Egypt, one of the world's major granaries at the time. Many of the tools and methods employed then are still in use in different parts of the world today.*

RIGHT *The Temple and Step Pyramid at Saqqara near modern Cairo. The temples of Egypt and the pyramid tombs of the pharaohs – divine kings – symbolized the absolute authority of the rulers and are now part of the most popular image of the country.*

vinced that God had chosen him to lead his people away from Egyptian rule to found a new nation. According to the Book of Exodus, Moses and his brother Aaron used the famous plagues to prove that the Hebrew God was more powerful than all the Egyptian gods, and forced the Egyptian Pharaoh to release the Hebrews.

The escape started with a celebration of the Passover, which was—and still is—the main Hebrew festival to which the other feasts are linked. Originally a protection rite for nomadic shepherds, Passover became the main commemoration of God's power to save his worshippers from any danger, and of his covenant with them.

The Covenant

Pursued by Egyptian soldiers, the Hebrews threw off the Egyptians in the salt marshes of the 'Sea of Reeds' (a better translation than 'Red Sea') and escaped into the desert areas east of the Nile delta. In order to avoid Egyptian troops on the coastal routes, and to reach the remote grazing lands of the nomadic shepherd tribes to which they were related, they turned south into the Sinai Peninsula.

Deep in the Sinai Peninsula, the Hebrews received the covenant with God at a sacred mountain. This confirmed their beliefs that the escape from Egypt was the supreme man-

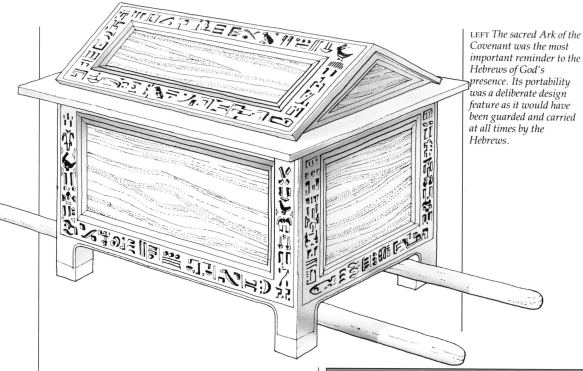

LAND OF GOSHEN

Heracleopo

R. N

ifestation of God's power and of his choice of them to be his special priestly people. For the Hebrews, these events gave ultimate authority to all their worship and law, by which they could express their gratitude and obedience to the God who had saved them.

Sacred Events

The Bible is essentially a record of sacred events rather than a book of abstract theological writings, and in each of its two major sections—the Old and New Testaments—there is an outstanding event to which everything else is related.

The escape from Egypt, the Exodus, is the outstanding event of the Old Testament, and the crucifixion and resurrection of Jesus form the corresponding event for the New Testament. The Bible makes it clear that neither of these events was fully understood at the time when they happened. The Exodus took place about 1250 BC, but it was at least seven centuries before the Hebrew people realized its full significance as a message of salvation to all the world. The crucifixion took place about AD 30, but some of the New Testament writers were still interpreting its significance nearly 70 years later.

ABOVE *Mount Sinai, deep in the southern Sinai Peninsula where the Hebrews received their covenant from God. The sacred mountain is now guarded by a fortified monastery.*

RIGHT *The escape, or exodus, of the Hebrews, led by Moses, from Egypt occurred in about 1250 BC through the marshes near the Mediterranean coast to the east of the Nile delta. The vicissitudes of the journey south through the Sinai Peninsula helped to forge the Hebrew identity.*

—— *Route of exodus*

—— *Major trade routes*

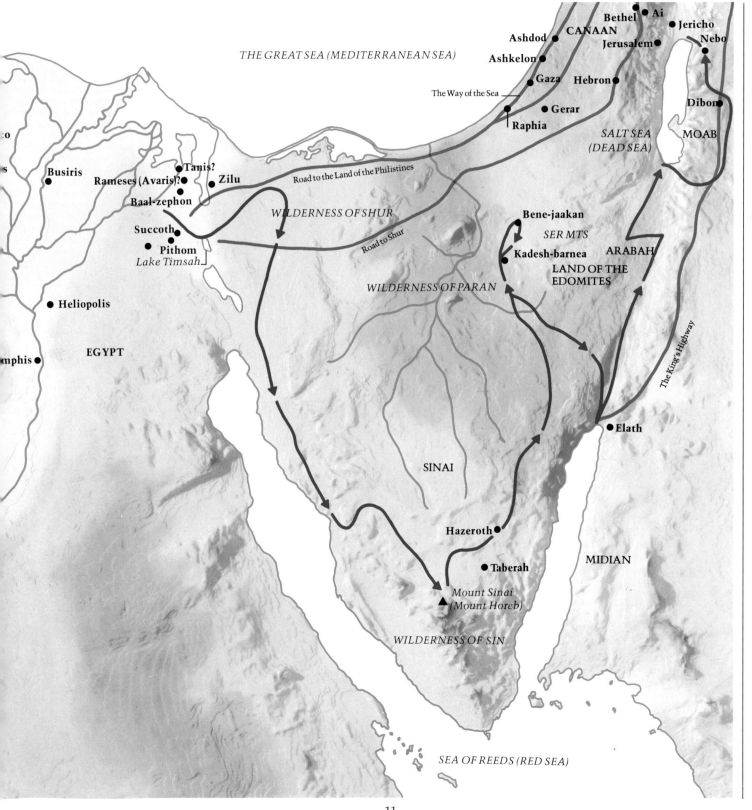

Bethel
Ai
CANAAN
Jericho
Ashdod
Jerusalem
Nebo
Ashkelon
THE GREAT SEA (MEDITERRANEAN SEA)
Gaza
Hebron
The Way of the Sea
Dibon
Raphia
Gerar
SALT SEA
(DEAD SEA)
MOAB
Busiris
Tanis?
Zilu
Rameses (Avaris)?
Road to the Land of the Philistines
Baal-zephon
WILDERNESS OF SHUR
Bene-jaakan
Succoth
Road to Shur
SER MTS
Pithom
Kadesh-barnea
ARABAH
Lake Timsah
LAND OF THE
EDOMITES
WILDERNESS OF PARAN
Heliopolis
The King's Highway
EGYPT
mphis
Elath
SINAI
Hazeroth
MIDIAN
Taberah
Mount Sinai
(Mount Horeb)
WILDERNESS OF SIN
SEA OF REEDS (RED SEA)

A Communal Work

The contents of the Bible, as we know it, passed through many hands before it was written down. The stories were shared and preserved by word of mouth, together with explanations and comments which related them to ordinary, everyday life. They were part of the communal experience of history and of worship, which traced the effects of God's saving acts in the lives of the people who felt they had been influenced by them. There are no 'simple' descriptions of what happened, for they all reflect the beliefs of the people who recorded them, and are an integral part of those beliefs.

Consequently, it is difficult to say precisely when any part of the Bible was written, or when exactly the contents were edited into the book we now have. It is more important to appreciate the kind of lives the people lived, the countries they inhabited and the forces which shaped their societies. This is now easier to do, as archaeology uncovers more of the past and confirms the picture presented to us by the ancient biblical records.

ABOVE *Their escape from Egypt convinced the Hebrews of their own salvation and that God was more powerful even than the Egyptian gods represented by the great pyramids.*

RIGHT *The ancient port of Tyre linked the Near and Middle East with the Mediterranean world.*

Centres of Civilization

In ancient times, the two great centres of civilization in the middle east were located in Egypt and Mesopotamia. Between them lay parched desert and the Dead Sea, and the narrow land of Palestine which formed the only viable route for armies, trade and the nomadic shepherd peoples. Consequently, Palestine was always at the centre of international tension and strife.

South of Palestine lay Egypt traversed by the River Nile draining the tropics of eastern Africa. The rich agricultural lands made the area the most important source of food in the eastern Mediterranean. The people who drained the Nile marshes and maintained the irrigation canals created one of the oldest civilizations of the ancient world, whose engineering skills can still be admired 50 centuries later in the impressive ruins of pyramids and temples.

Beyond the Syrian and Arabian desert, east of Palestine, lay Mesopotamia, drained by the rivers Tigris and Euphrates. There too, civilizations arose from the skills learned in controlling the river floods and turning

The Holy Land

Palestine gets its name from the Philistines who briefly controlled the narrow land-bridge at the end of the second millenium BC when they conquered it from the sea. The conquered natives were Canaanites living in independent, isolated hill fortresses. By 1000 BC the Hebrews had conquered both the Philistines and Canaanites to form the brief empire of Kings David and Solomon. For the Hebrews, this success was the final stage of the escape from Egypt and God's fulfilment of his covenant with them; from then onwards this would be the Holy Land.

The main international route from Egypt passed northward along the coast of Palestine to the ridge of Mount Carmel, where it split into an eastern branch to Syria and Mesopotamia. This branch skirted the Sea of Galilee while the western branch went to Tyre and Asia Minor. Palestine derived its prosperity and insecurity from this vital road and also exposed the Hebrews to an enormous range of cultural influences.

Apart from trade and war—for they were renowned mercenary soldiers—the Hebrews

them to agricultural needs. Despite its teeming population and great military powers, Mesopotamia was vulnerable to invasion from the mountain tribes to the east, so no single city or dynasty was supreme for long. As in Egypt, power in Mesopotamia moved up and down the river valleys.

Throughout this 'fertile crescent' from the Persian Gulf to Egypt, nomadic shepherds drove their flocks through the marginal lands between desert and the river valleys, owing allegience to no one, amongst them were the Hebrews.

ABOVE *Palestine became the 'Holy Land' and the Hebrew sanctuaries there were some of the holiest places of all.*

+ *Major sanctuaries associated with the Hebrews of Gen 12–50*

— *Major trade routes*

① *The Way of the Sea*

② *The King's Highway*

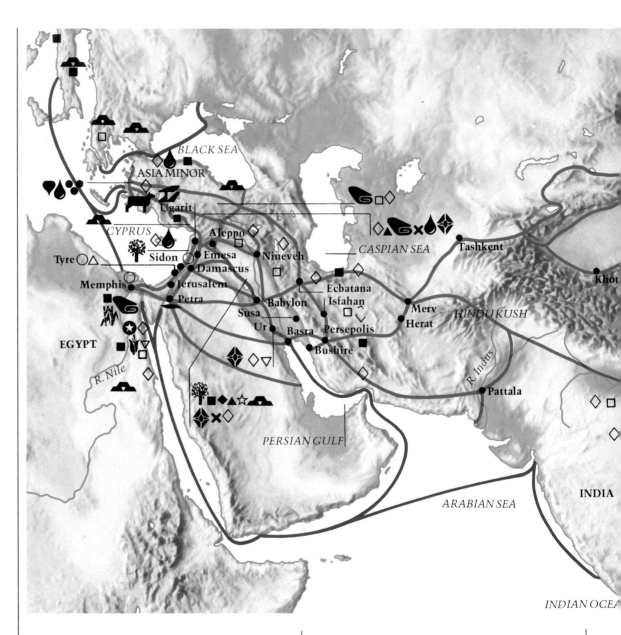

RIGHT *The reliance of traders on pack animals to transport their merchandise tended to limit the major trade routes – which are particularly concentrated in and around Palestine – to areas of land which most readily supported life.*

	'Fertile crescent'
	Major land trade routes
	Major maritime trade routes
○	Glassware
◈	Precious stones
◢	Asphalt
♦	Corn
◗	Olive Oil
⚒	Metals
✕	Donkeys
♥	Figs
✒	Silk
◗◗	Wine
◖	Textiles
▰	Gold
◇	Copper
□	Tin
🌳	Wood
■	Iron
✪	Frankincense
△	Dyes (especially purple)
▲	lead
▽	Ivory
🜨	Papyrus
🐑	Wool
◆	Bronze
☆	Silver

of ancient Palestine fell into two economic groups: the nomadic shepherds leading mobile lives, and the settled farmers of the fortified agricultural towns. As the Hebrews strengthened their hold over Palestine they turned more and more to farming. The change had profound consequences for their social and political patterns, and also for their religion.

The fortified settlements of the farming communities had a social structure based on land ownership, with pyramids of power capped by the kings of the various 'cities'.

The bulk of the peple existed as landless slaves owned by the farming and military classes, and all of them ruled by kings with absolute powers. As the Hebrews became farmers, so they turned to this way of life.

The New Way of Life

The Canaanite farmers of Palestine worshipped a host of gods and goddesses all related to the needs of a farming community. The

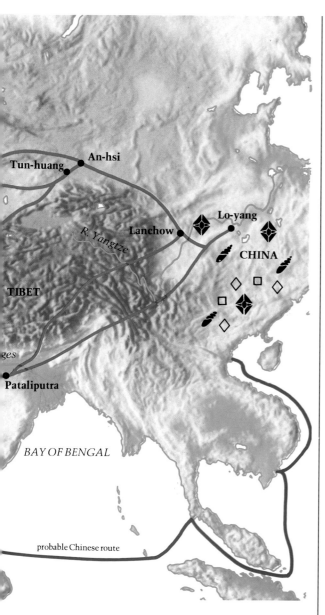

ABOVE *The cultivation and drainage of the marshes of the Rivers Tigris and Euphrates were important early stages in the civilizations of Mesopotamia.*

main theme was the fertility of the land, which was secured by the sexual intercourse between the gods and goddesses. This was re-enacted between priests, priestesses and people in religious rites to ensure the fertility of the crops. Human sacrifice was also practised to secure the fertility of the fields or to avert military disaster. The main festivals were associated with the cycle of the agricultural year, from sowing to harvest. Each city had its temple, and there were sanctuaries in groves of trees and on hills.

As the Hebrews became farmers, they turned to this type of religion which seemed so necessary to life in Canaan. Much of the Old Testament is concerned with the struggle to adapt the Hebrew religion of the Exodus and covenant to the new way of life. As nomadic shepherds, the Hebrews had lived as close-knit families which formed the basis for clans and tribes. There was little difference of class where the flocks belonged to the whole family, and the heads of families were the natural patriarch-rulers.

The old Hebrew religion of the Exodus emphasized God as Father, and the essential quality and value of everyone in the community, for all of them were 'people of the covenant'. They worshipped at a portable shrine, the 'ark of the covenant', which they carried with them and there was no separate priestly class. Eventually the two systems of belief were reconciled and the old Hebrew religious values prevailed, but only after centuries of struggle during which prophets withstood (endured) the corruption of Hebrew kings and priests, often at the cost of their lives.

The Fertile Country

The great hill fortress of Megiddo is typical of many Canaanite cities, and of Hebrew cities after the Canaanites had been conquered. Like Jerusalem, Megiddo's thick walls and cunningly (cleverly) designed gate defended a rocky hill with storage pits for grain and a shaft and tunnel which gave access to the city's water supply during times when the city was besieged.

As in Egypt and Mesopotamia, the main crops of Palestine were wheat and barley, commemorated in the feasts of Unleavened Bread and Weeks (Pentecost). Dates, olives, grapes, citrus and a range of other fruits and vegetables were cultivated wherever water was found or land irrigated. Almost everywhere in Palestine is fertile if water can be provided, and excavations have shown that far more of the country was cultivated, through elaborate irrigation schemes, than was once thought possible.

Even near the Dead Sea, freshwater springs made for tropical luxury in such ancient centres as Jericho. The springs made it possible to maintain comfortable settle-

ABOVE *The Canaanite farmers of Palestine believed that the fertility of their fields depended on the faithful worship of the Caananite fertility gods and goddesses.*

FAR RIGHT *The code of Hammurabi, King of Babylonia during the 17th century BC, was one of the most influential codes of laws in the ancient Middle East.*

RIGHT *Southern Palestine is relatively arid compared to the north where the mountains catch the rain carried by the westerly winds. The rainfall in the mountains runs off into the Jordan valley.*

ments on the western shores of the Dead Sea in biblical times. Where springs were lacking or inadequate, the inhabitants dammed the deep gullies of the rift valley through which the River Jordan flows to the Dead Sea. The water was then channelled to their towns. We can begin to see why the Bible describes Palestine as 'a land of wheat and barley, of vines, of figs, of pomegranates, a land of olives, of oil, of honey. . . a land where stones are of iron, where the hills may be quarried for copper. . . where your flocks and herds increase'.

The Struggle for Palestine

But the people of Palestine, whether Canaanites or Hebrews, were seldom left in peace. As the patterns of domination waxed and waned in Mesopotomia and Egypt, Palestine usually found itself a centre of contention as one power or another saw it as a frontier area essential to its security. It was free from occupation by foreign powers less than 200 years out of 2,000.

In Mesopotamia, the Sumerian civilization

THE GREAT SEA
(MEDITERRANEAN SEA)

ASIA MINOR

MESOPOTAMIA →

Damascus

Jezzine

Mount
Hermon

Tyre

Dan

Lake Huleh

Hazor

Acco

SEA OF CHINNERETH
(SEA OF GALILEE)

Mount Carmel

Nazareth

Ashtaroth

Wadi Yarmuk

Megiddo

Beth-shan

Aruna

Jezreel

Ramoth-gilead

PLAIN OF
SHARON

Jenin

HILL COUNTRY
OF EPHRAIM

Samaria

Mahanaim

Shechem

Joppa

Aphek

Shiloh

R. Jordan

Bethel

Rabbah

Jericho

Ekron

Heshbon

Ashdod
Gath?

Jerusalem
(Jebus)

Ashkelon

Bethlehem

SHEPHELAH

Zereth-shahar

HILL COUNTRY
OF JUDAH

Gaza

Eglon

Lachish

Hebron

En-gedi

Dibon

PLAIN OF
PHILISTIA

SALT SEA
(DEAD SEA)

Beer-sheba

Kir-hareseth

EGYPT

THE NEGEB

---	Regional rainfall:	④	Above 50in (1300mm)	④	The Eastern Hills
①	0–15in (0–400mm)	---	Natural regions:	⑤	The Desert
②	15–30in (400–800mm)	①	The Coastal Plain	ⓐ	The Way of the Sea
③	30–50in (800–1300mm)	②	The Western Hills	ⓑ	The King's Highway
		③	The Rift Valley		

was already in decline when Abraham left her borders in about 1800 BC. Babylon was rising as the dominant power under the leadership of King Hammurabi, and soon conquered every district of Mesopotamia and Syria from the Gulf to the Mediterranean. The Babylonians failed to penetrate into Palestine as Egypt strengthened its hold over the Canaanite cities. Before they were overthrown by the Kassites, they left a legacy of a great legal code and epic religious myths. The Babylonian creation legends and the 'Epic of Gilgamesh' undoubtedly influenced the opening chapters of the Book of Genesis, even though the Hebrew authors transformed the materials as they used them.

Contending Powers

For a brief period, around the time of the Hebrew migration to Egypt, the Hittites of

Asia Minor seemed set to dominate the area north of Palestine. Egyptian control was sustained, particularly by the Hyksos rulers, and the contending powers of Mesopotamia, including the Assyrians, were too weak to challenge Egypt. The time came when the Assyrians conquered the whole of the middle east, but this was not until five centuries after the Hebrew escape from Egypt.

Egypt might have taken advantage of the struggle for power in Mesopotamia during the period between Abraham and the Hebrew Exodus, the middle part of the second millenium BC, but she was torn by internal strife. For nearly a century, northern Egypt and Palestine were ruled by the invading Hyksos, but even when the native Egyptians regained control there was no internal stability for long.

The Religion of Egypt

As religion played such a central part in Egyptian life, so too it was a focus for power struggles. Although the Egyptian king was worshipped as the divine mediator between the gods and the people of Egypt, the priests of the many gods exercised enormous power as the country's administrators and intellectuals.

The main theme in Egyptian religion, expressed particularly in the architecture and orientation of pyramids, stelae and temples, was the worship of the sun. The rising of the sun was the source of creation and renewal, while the journey of the sun god through the underworld during the night reflected the pattern of death and regeneration. It was a religion full of meaning for an agricultural people.

About a century before the Hebrew exodus from Egypt, King Akhnaton tried to impose a single, uniform religion and government on the people of Egypt by suppressing all expressions of religion except the worship of the sun. The priests defeated his attempts at religious reform and the monuments to his monotheism were defaced after his death, possibly during the rein of the young Tut'ankhamun. Egypt never succeeded in extending her power far beyond her borders because of the problem of maintaining internal unity.

ABOVE *The sphinx was a mythical beast, a composite of a lion's body and a human head. The head of the Great Sphinx is that of King Knafra of the 4th dynasty.*

Origins

BELOW *The Great Sphinx at Al Jizah, sculpted from natural rock, is perhaps the single most monumental expression of the divine authority of the rulers of ancient Egypt, although its original meaning is not altogether clear.*

Philistines

As the Hebrews, newly escaped from Egypt, wound their way through the desert areas south of the Dead Sea towards Palestine, near the end of the thirteenth century BC, the region was unusually free from control by any of the great international powers.

Normally, Egypt kept a close watch over Canaan (soon to become known as 'The Land of the Philistines' — Palestine) through client states and military patrols, but the Philistines were attacking Egypt from the sea and the Egyptians were fully occupied in repulsing them. The Philistines successfully invaded Canaan, and established five cities as their base—Gaza, Ashkelon, Ashdod, Gath and Ekron—before imposing their rule over the rest of the country. Egypt was powerless to interfere as she was weakened by internal conflicts between the Pharaoh and the powerful, wealthy groups of priests who controlled local districts of Egypt.

The great states to the north of Palestine, in Asia Minor, and to the east in Mesopotamia failed to take advantage of Egyptian weakness and control Palestine; they too were incapa-

BELOW *The ancient Egyptians defeated the Sea Peoples or Philistines at a great naval battle, but they could not stop them from establishing themselves in Palestine.*

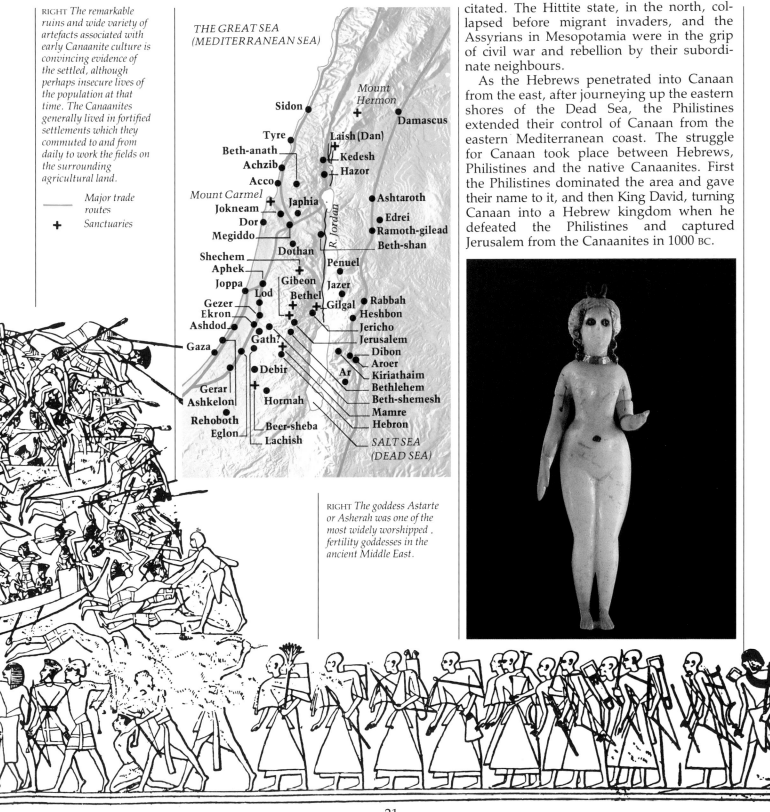

RIGHT *The remarkable ruins and wide variety of artefacts associated with early Canaanite culture is convincing evidence of the settled, although perhaps insecure lives of the population at that time. The Canaanites generally lived in fortified settlements which they commuted to and from daily to work the fields on the surrounding agricultural land.*

——— Major trade routes

+ Sanctuaries

THE GREAT SEA (MEDITERRANEAN SEA)

Mount Hermon

Sidon
Damascus
Tyre
Laish (Dan)
Beth-anath
Kedesh
Achzib
Hazor
Acco
Mount Carmel
Ashtaroth
Jokneam
Japhia
Dor
Edrei
Megiddo
Ramoth-gilead
Dothan
Beth-shan
R. Jordan
Shechem
Penuel
Aphek
Joppa
Gibeon
Jazer
Lod
Bethel
Gezer
Gilgal
Rabbah
Ekron
Heshbon
Ashdod
Jericho
Gath?
Jerusalem
Gaza
Dibon
Aroer
Debir
Kiriathaim
Ar
Bethlehem
Beth-shemesh
Gerar
Mamre
Ashkelon
Hormah
Hebron
Rehoboth
Beer-sheba
Eglon
Lachish
SALT SEA (DEAD SEA)

RIGHT *The goddess Astarte or Asherah was one of the most widely worshipped fertility goddesses in the ancient Middle East.*

citated. The Hittite state, in the north, collapsed before migrant invaders, and the Assyrians in Mesopotamia were in the grip of civil war and rebellion by their subordinate neighbours.

As the Hebrews penetrated into Canaan from the east, after journeying up the eastern shores of the Dead Sea, the Philistines extended their control of Canaan from the eastern Mediterranean coast. The struggle for Canaan took place between Hebrews, Philistines and the native Canaanites. First the Philistines dominated the area and gave their name to it, and then King David, turning Canaan into a Hebrew kingdom when he defeated the Philistines and captured Jerusalem from the Canaanites in 1000 BC.

Canaanites

The Canaanites whom the Hebrews conquered were a mixture of peoples, from the seafaring Phoenicians of the northern coast to the farmers of the south, but there was a strong cultural unity among them. Compared with the Hebrews they were advanced in technology and literature. Canaanite scribes developed the first true alphabet, which passed from pictorial writing to the more flexible single-letter scripts which were eventually adopted throughout the middle east and, in due course, the world. Its secret was the use of vocal sounds, the smallest components of words, as the basic units for the alphabetical scripts.

The Canaanite way of life, including their religion, revolved round the basic needs of farming and defence. They worshipped a complex pantheon of gods and goddesses, of whom the most important were El, the father of the Gods, and the goddess Asherah. Baal, son of El and Asherah, is frequently denounced in the Old Testament as a threat to the purity of Hebrew religion, a sure indication that many Hebrews were attracted by Canaanite worship.

City-States

Like the Greeks in their city-states, the Canaanite cities were frequently at war with each other, and Canaanite history reveals a shifting pattern of alliances and enmities between the various small states. The Canaanite cities were hill-top strongholds, heavily fortified against other Canaanite cities, scattered across the parts of Palestine capable of being farmed. With no central organization or government, the Canaanites fell first to the Philistines and then to the Hebrews.

The Hebrews were deeply influenced by the Canaanite way of life. They adopted some of the language and symbolism of Canaanite religion, particularly the name El for God, and aspects of the Canaanite creation stories. As Hebrew worship developed, it adopted rites and festivals associated with the Canaanite agricultural year: the main harvest festivals (which the Hebrews then related to the power God had demonstrated when he rescued them from the Egyptians), and the sacrifice of animals, crops and incense as burnt offerings and communion meals.

The Old Testament roundly condemns the Canaanite fertility rites as sacred prostitution, and the terrible sacrifice of children to the god Molech. It is clear that these practices were widespread among Hebrews as they adopted the Canaanite way of life. During the height of the Hebrew monarchy a shrine to Molech was built outside Jerusalem, and at least two of the Hebrew kings sacrificed their sons there in times of national danger.

	OX	HOUSE
EGYPTIAN HIEROGLYPHICS c3000 BC		
CANAANITE c2000 BC		
PHOENICIAN c1000 BC		
HEBREW c700 BC		
OLD GREEK c650 BC		
ARAMAIC c350 BC		
FORMAL HEBREW c150 BC		
FORMAL GREEK c450 BC		
ROMAN c550 BC		

ABOVE *The Canaanite scribes invented the first alphabet, from which all Western systems of writing were derived.*

WATER	EYE	HEAD	PAPYRUS	
				Egyptian writing did not develop far from the use of pictorial symbols.
				Canaanite writing shows its pictorial origins, but in fact symbolizes basic sounds.
				The 22 basic symbols of the Canaanite system became the standard for the region.
				The Hebrews adopted the Canaanite alphabet in a modified form.
				The Canaanite origins can still be seen in archaic Greek script.
				Aramaic was the main language of the Persian Empire, and displaced Hebrew in Palestine.
				Classical Hebrew was written in a 'square' form of the common script of the region.
				The Greek alphabet allocated vowel sounds to some of the letters, and added more symbols.
				The Romans gained their alphabet from the Etruscans and Greek colonists.

RIGHT *The strength of the fortifications which constitute the ancient fort of Jericho (Hebrew for 'fragrant') were dramatically revealed when archaeologists unearthed one of the great corner forts of its walls.*

Temples

The architecture of Canaanite temples strongly influenced Hebrew religious buildings. The excavations at the temple in Hazor in northern Palestine reveal a succession of rectangular rooms leading to a large, innermost sanctuary with a carved square altar displaying the symbol of the storm god, Baal, and a seated statue. Two pillars situated between the temple porch and the middle chamber served no structural purpose and must have been used in the Canaanite religious rites. This pattern is very similar to the Temple King Solomon built in Jerusalem as

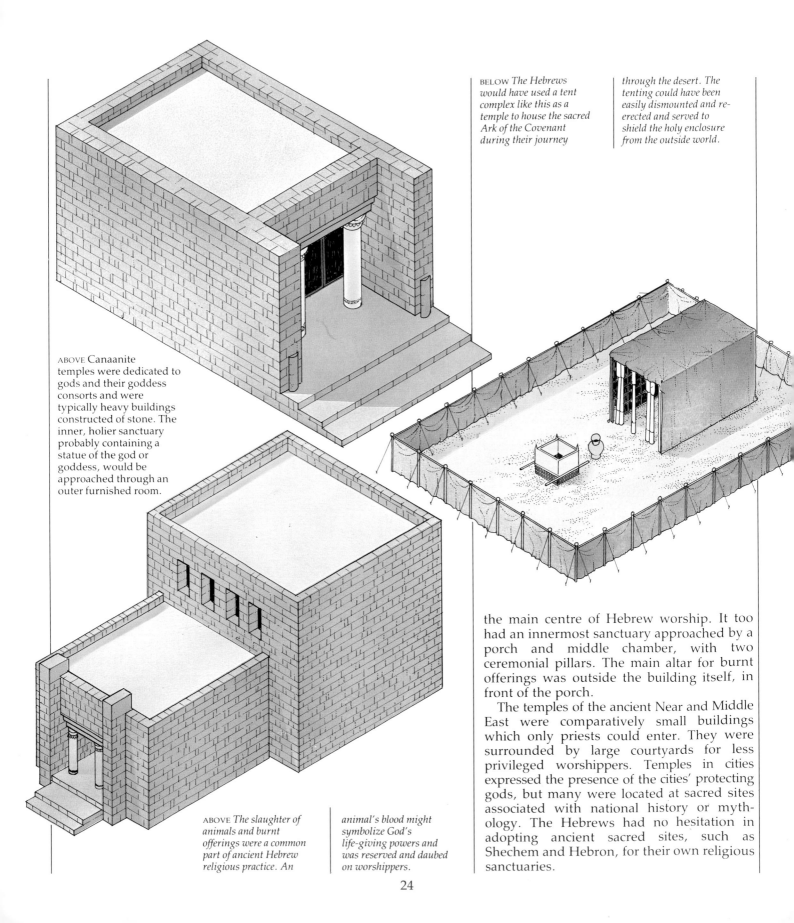

BELOW *The Hebrews would have used a tent complex like this as a temple to house the sacred Ark of the Covenant during their journey* *through the desert. The tenting could have been easily dismounted and re-erected and served to shield the holy enclosure from the outside world.*

ABOVE Canaanite temples were dedicated to gods and their goddess consorts and were typically heavy buildings constructed of stone. The inner, holier sanctuary probably containing a statue of the god or goddess, would be approached through an outer furnished room.

ABOVE *The slaughter of animals and burnt offerings were a common part of ancient Hebrew religious practice. An* *animal's blood might symbolize God's life-giving powers and was reserved and daubed on worshippers.*

the main centre of Hebrew worship. It too had an innermost sanctuary approached by a porch and middle chamber, with two ceremonial pillars. The main altar for burnt offerings was outside the building itself, in front of the porch.

The temples of the ancient Near and Middle East were comparatively small buildings which only priests could enter. They were surrounded by large courtyards for less privileged worshippers. Temples in cities expressed the presence of the cities' protecting gods, but many were located at sacred sites associated with national history or mythology. The Hebrews had no hesitation in adopting ancient sacred sites, such as Shechem and Hebron, for their own religious sanctuaries.

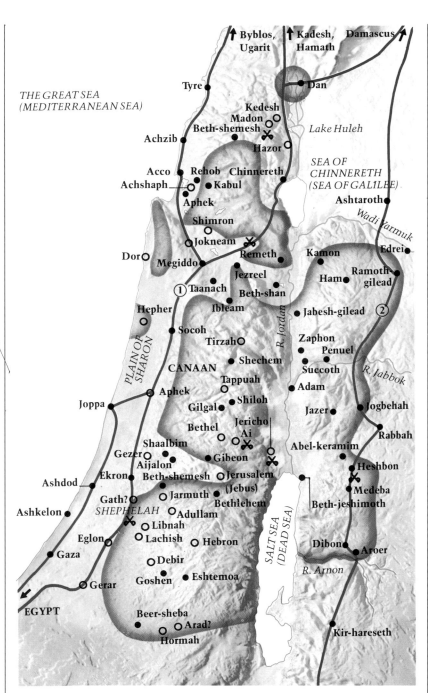

THE GREAT SEA
(MEDITERRANEAN SEA)

↑ Byblos, Ugarit   ↑ Kadesh, Hamath   Damascus ↑

Tyre
Dan
Kedesh
Madon
Beth-shemesh
Achzib
Lake Huleh
Hazor
SEA OF CHINNERETH (SEA OF GALILEE)
Acco
Rehob   Chinnereth
Achshaph
Kabul
Ashtaroth
Aphek
Wadi Yarmuk
Shimron
Jokneam
Remeth
Kamon
Edrei
Dor
Megiddo
Jezreel
Ham
Ramoth-gilead
① Taanach
Beth-shan
Hepher
Ibleam
Jabesh-gilead ②
Socoh
Zaphon
Tirzah
Penuel
CANAAN
Shechem
Succoth
R. Jabbok
Tappuah
Adam
Aphek
Shiloh
Gilgal
Jazer
Jogbehah
Bethel
Jericho
Ai
Shaalbim
Abel-keramim
Rabbah
Gezer
Gibeon
Aijalon
Heshbon
Ekron
Beth-shemesh
Jerusalem (Jebus)
Ashdod
Jarmuth
Bethlehem
Medeba
Gath?
Adullam
Beth-jeshimoth
SHEPHELAH
Ashkelon
Libnah
Eglon
Lachish   Hebron
Dibon
Aroer
Gaza
Debir
R. Arnon
Gerar
Goshen   Eshtemoa
EGYPT
Beer-sheba
Arad?
Kir-hareseth
Hormah

PLAIN OF SHARON
R. Jordan
SALT SEA (DEAD SEA)
Joppa

ABOVE The Hebrews infiltrated Canaan only gradually, at first occupying the most sparsely populated land neglected by the Canaanites. Once the Hebrews were settled, numerous and united enough, they began to overrun the cities, a trend the poorly organized Canaanites could do very little about.

○   Conquered cities

——   Major trade routes

①   The Way of the Sea

②   The King's Highway

✂   Sites of conflicts

  Regions of early Hebrew settlements

Divine Rights

The Book of Joshua presents a dramatic account of the Hebrew conquest of Palestine. A more difficult consolidation period followed, which is recorded in the Book of Judges, when the Philistines controlled the land. These accounts emphasize that God had given the land to the Hebrews, and that national security depended on strict obedience and loyalty to God. The divine rights of the Hebrew people as God's chosen are a prominent theme, both here and in other Old Testament writings.

An analysis of the lists of Canaanite cities and kings given in the Book of Joshua (places conquered by the Hebrews, places where they failed, and lists of the territories eventually allocated to the various Hebrew tribes) show that the occupation proceeded in three phases.

First the Hebrews took Jericho in the Jordan Valley, and then they moved into the Judean hill country south of Jerusalem. At this stage Jerusalem was too strong to capture and it did not become a Hebrew city until two centuries later when King David made it his capital. In the next phase they took the hill country north of Jerusalem, and the coastal plain of Sharon north of Joppa. Finally, there were the wars of the northern cities, including the great trading centre of Hazor on the road to Damascus and Mesopotamia.

Subjugation

The campaign was more of an infiltration than a conquest, in which the Hebrews neutralized Canaanite opposition as they occupied the marginal lands between the city territories, by defeating coalitions of Canaanite kings. In all, the full occupation took a century and a half to complete, and was not secure until the Hebrews defeated the Philistines in the time of King David. Until they adopted Canaanite farming methods, the nomadic Hebrew shepherds could co-exist with the Canaanite farming settlements, as they were not competing for the agricultural land. By the time of David, the Hebrew way of life had changed so much

that they had to subjugate the Canaanites and Philistines, or be subjugated by them. This is the true significance of King David's success, and the source of his outstanding reputation as the founder of the main Hebrew dynasty.

The Book of Judges tells of the deeds of 12 'judges', who rallied various combinations of the Hebrew tribes and organized them to resist attacks by the Canaanites or enemies beyond the borders of Palestine. Their success in a military crisis gave them extraordinary authority as people filled with God's power and wisdom, and they continued to exercise this authority after peace had been restored. For most of this period the Hebrews continued to live as independent tribes with no central organization to unite them, except for the central sanctuaries where the sacred Hebrew Ark of the Covenant was housed at

ABOVE *The heavily fortified Canaanite hill-top cities were the last pockets of resistance in Palestine to fall to the Hebrews.*

various times, particularly Shechem and Shiloh. The Hebrew tribes who settled in the northern parts of Palestine seem to have had little contact with those settled in Judah, who adopted Hebron as their main sanctuary, and between the two there was a belt of Canaanite cities, including Jerusalem, where the Hebrews had not established a foothold.

Enemies

Apart from the Canaanites, who were too weakened by inter-city wars to dislodge the Hebrews, other enemies of the Hebrews are named as the Edomites, Moabites and Ammonites. They were located on the international route which passed northwards along

the eastern side of the Dead Sea and the Jordan valley. This was the route taken by the Hebrews on their way to Palestine from Egypt, and was the traditional route for the nomadic shepherds. The Midianites are named as another enemy, and since this was the nomadic tribe which had helped the Hebrews during their escape from Egypt, mention of them shows that the Hebrews had become settled people who had begun to resent the incursions of nomadic shepherds!

With the final chapters of the Book of Joshua, and the First Book of Samuel, the history reaches the struggles of the Hebrews against the Philistines as they tightened their control of Palestine from the Philistine coastal cities of Gaza, Ashkelon, Ashdod, Gath and Ekron. In these stories, Samson is the most colourful of the judges, even though he was eventually unsuccessful against the Phili-

ABOVE *David had to flee for safety to the desert region of Judah to escape Saul's jealousy.*

stines. Behind the vivid folk legends, we can glimpse a resistance fighter who organized a small guerrilla war against the Philistines in the hill country of Judah, and was not afraid to penetrate occasionally into the Philistine strongholds themselves.

At the central sanctuary of Shiloh, north of Jerusalem, the Ark of the Covenant was tended by a Hebrew priestly family, headed by Eli. Here the young Samuel was dedicated to the service of the shrine by his parents. Samuel would have been serving there when the Hebrews carried the sacred Ark into battle against the Philistines at Aphek, around the year 1050 BC. The Hebrews were defeated, the Philistines captured the Ark and Shiloh was destroyed. Samuel went on to be the last of the charismatic leaders of the Hebrews before the real emergence of the Hebrew monarchy.

Saul, the First King

Defeat by the Philistines showed the Hebrews that the old, informal federation of Hebrew tribes could no longer defend the people now that they had settled in permanent locations. They needed a recognized, central ruler, and Samuel organized the anointing of Saul as the first Hebrew king.

Perhaps the new form of government was too great a change, particularly while Samuel was still a powerful force, and Saul did not command the loyalty of the southern Hebrew tribes. Saul clashed with Samuel, and then was defeated by the Philistines near Mount Gilboa in the valley of Jezreel and committed suicide. David had served in Saul's court and had already acquired a powerful military reputation and a band of followers. Saul's death gave David his opportunity to become the king who first united the Hebrew people and gave them security by defeating the Philistines.

David

Bethlehem, the most northerly town in Judah and just south of Jerusalem, first became famous as the birthplace of David. It was from Bethlehem that the young David went to King Saul's court as a page and army officer. With King Saul's defeat by the Philistines and subsequent death, David was able to secure the support of both the northern and the southern groups of Hebrew tribes, and was anointed king in Saul's place by both groups.

David emerged as an astute politician of many talents. The lament he wrote for Saul and his son Jonathan after the Battle of Gilboa reveals David as the poet who wrote at least some of the psalms. David's political stature is shown by the skill with which he commanded the loyalty of the many different groups among the Hebrews. He finally reinforced his position as king of all the Hebrews by choosing as his capital a city which had no previous political or religious associations for any of the Hebrew tribes, Jerusalem.

RIGHT *David was the first king of a united Palestine and made Jerusalem, a neutral city, his capital. He was first accepted by the southern Hebrews and then by the northern tribes and with the nation behind him assumed firm control over the land of Israel and the trade routes passing through it. Carefully chosen governors ruled the subservient states outside the areas of David's direct rule.*

● *Philistine cities*

Sanctuaries during the early monarchy

+

◎ *Cities strengthened by King Solomon*

The Land of Israel

Conquered region under Israel's rule

Region under vassal treaty

—— *Major trade routes*

LEFT *The Gihon spring was ancient Jerusalem's only water supply and essential to the city's successful defence. David's troops eventually captured the city by entering via the spring's access shaft.*

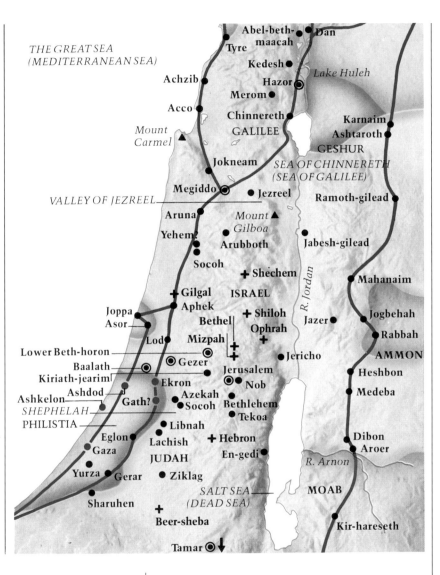

THE GREAT SEA
(MEDITERRANEAN SEA)

Abel-beth-maacah • Dan
Tyre •
Kedesh •
Achzib • Hazor ◎ Lake Huleh
Merom •
Acco • Chinnereth Karnaim
Mount GALILEE Ashtaroth
Carmel ▲ GESHUR
Jokneam SEA OF CHINNERETH
(SEA OF GALILEE)
Megiddo ◎ • Jezreel
VALLEY OF JEZREEL Ramoth-gilead
Aruna Mount ▲
Yehem Gilboa
• Arubboth Jabesh-gilead
Socoh
+ Shechem Mahanaim
+ Gilgal ISRAEL
Aphek + Shiloh Jogbehah
Joppa Bethel Ophrah Jazer • Rabbah
Asor + +
Lod Mizpah Jericho AMMON
Lower Beth-horon + + Heshbon
◎ Gezer Jerusalem
Baalath ◎ ◎ • Nob Medeba
Kiriath-jearim Ekron Bethlehem
Ashkelon Ashdod Azekah •
Gath? • Socoh • Tekoa
SHEPHELAH Libnah + Hebron Dibon
PHILISTIA Eglon Lachish Aroer
Gaza • En-gedi R. Arnon
Yurza JUDAH
Gerar • Ziklag SALT SEA MOAB
Sharuhen (DEAD SEA)
+ Kir-hareseth
Beer-sheba
Tamar ◎ ↓

R. Jordan

David captured Jerusalem from its Canaanite citizens and made it the national religious centre for Hebrews by installing the sacred Ark of the Covenant in it.

By defeating the Philistines, King David not only gave his people national security in Palestine, he also gained control of the great international trade routes which had to pass through the area. He established his rule from Damascus to the Egyptian border, and from the Great Sea (the Mediterranean) to the Syrian desert. The Hebrews had won a small empire centred on Palestine. David's descendants inherited his throne by divine right as guardians of the covenant with God, and for the first time the Hebrews could look forward to a secure future.

Solomon's Temple

That future was not without its problems, particularly about religion. From the time of David's son and successor, King Solomon, tensions began to emerge between Hebrews who remained loyal to the old religion of the desert and the nomadic shepherds, and Hebrews who accepted the new political, economic and social structures. Much of this tension was focused on the new Temple built by Solomon in Jerusalem to house the Ark of the Covenant. The Temple symbolized the change from the old nomadic religion when the Ark travelled with the tribes in its own tent, to this new religion of settlements.

The new Temple in Jerusalem showed that at least some Hebrews had adopted the Canaanite way of life, with its fortified cities, its agricultural economy and its monarchical form of government. The Temple was not only the shrine of the Ark, it was also the royal chapel administered by priests who were appointed by the king.

The plan of the Temple confirmed this, for it was very similar to other temples in Canaanite areas. A small building, it was at most 150 feet (50 m) long by 60 feet (20 m) wide, and stood in the great court of the royal place with its own inner court. The two connecting chambers of porch and main hall led on into the innermost shrine which housed the Ark of the Covenant.

ABOVE *The imposing site of the great Temple built by Solomon on The Dome of the Rock in Jerusalem is now occupied by an impressively beautiful Islamic shrine.*

The Great Altar

The main hall contained an altar for burning incense, a table for the 'bread of the presence', and 10 lampstands. The main focus for worship stood in front of the Temple building, the great bronze altar of whole burnt offerings, a raised hearth 30 feet (10 m) square and 15 feet (5 m) high, on which the main sacrifices were made. The sacrificial animals, slaughtered nearby where channels drained away the blood, were carried by priests up a flight of steps to the fire which burnt perpetually on the altar. Near the altar was a bronze water basin 15 feet (5 m) in diameter and 8 feet (2.5 m) tall, and 10 wheeled

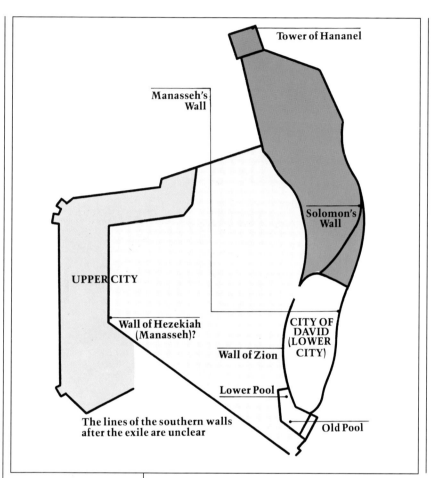

Tower of Hananel

Manasseh's Wall

Solomon's Wall

UPPER CITY

Wall of Hezekiah (Manasseh)?

CITY OF DAVID (LOWER CITY)

Wall of Zion

Lower Pool

The lines of the southern walls after the exile are unclear

Old Pool

ABOVE *The original Canaanite city of Jerusalem before its conquest by David. The city sat on a narrow ridge and was quite easily defended. Solomon built the Temple to house the Ark in the northern flatter part of the city.*

basins for carrying the water wherever it was needed in the Temple.

The architects of this first Hebrew Temple, and many of the workmen, were lent to King Solomon by the Canaanite King Hiram of Tyre, who also supplied the cedars for the pillars and the panelling. It survived for nearly 400 years, until the Babylonians destroyed it in 587 BC. Rebuilt by the Hebrews some 50 years later, after the Babylonian exile, the Temple was replaced magnificently by Herod the Great before and during the lifetime of Jesus, only to be destroyed during the Roman-Jewish War in AD 70. Since then it has never been replaced. Its site is now occupied by the oustandingly beautiful Moslem shrine, The Dome of the Rock.

A Golden Age

The Temple of Jerusalem and the royal palace were only some of the new buildings raised by King Solomon by the use of forced Hebrew labour. A number of Palestinian sites have the remains of massive fortifications constructed by Solomon, particularly Megiddo, Hazor and Gezer. The great shaft and tunnel at Megiddo, constructed to give safe access to the city's water supply in time of war, date from the time of Solomon or shortly after-

LEFT *The cultivators of the fields. The period of peace secured by Kings David and Solomon became a golden age of Hebrew prosperity.*

wards, as do the massive casemate walls and gateway of the city.

Solomon established an efficient central administration with reliable written records. He developed a thriving foreign trade along the land routes and by using a merchant fleet based on the Red Sea. Excavations have also uncovered evidence of a large-scale copper industry based on ore deposits in the Jordan Valley and in the Negev area, south of the Dead Sea. The prosperity created by Solomon's administration gave rise to a golden age for the Hebrew people and established Solomon's reputation for 'wisdom'. Clearly, Solomon could not have succeeded without a deep understanding of the new opportunities the time offered his people, and the skill to overcome the divisive tendencies of traditional Hebrew tribal loyalties. It is a measure of Solomon's abilities that the national unity forged by him and his father, King David, collapsed at Solomon's death in 931 BC.

Civil War

With the death of King Solomon the united Hebrew kingdom split into two kingdoms, a southern one, Judah, with Jerusalem as its capital, and a northern kingdom, Israel, with Samaria as its eventual capital. The descendants of David continued to rule Judah in an unbroken line for three and a half centuries, while the bloody history of Israel is marked by frequent changes of dynasty until it was destroyed by the Assyrians in 721 BC.

Shortly after the split, Egypt reasserted her control over Palestines when the Pharaoh Sheshonk marched an army through the area and stripped the Temple of its main treasures as tribute. Both the Hebrew kingdoms continued to exist, but in mutual enmity. The northern Hebrews were always far more prosperous and numerous than their southern brethren, and this difference increased as the northern kingdom benefitted from the trade routes which passed through it.

Golden Bulls

Differences in religious traditions added to contrasts in prosperity. Many Hebrews

RIGHT *Palestine was effectively at the nerve centre of a network of long-established trading routes and therefore ideally situated to take advantage of them once the Hebrews had overcome their enemies.*

——— Land routes
- - - - Sea routes

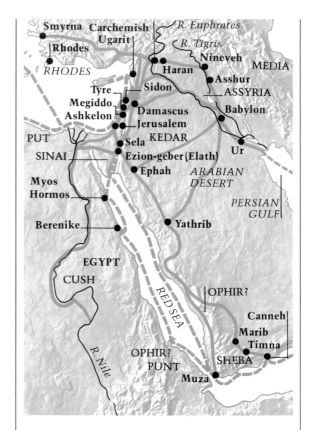

resented the change in emphasis exemplified by the new Temple in Jerusalem, especially as the old tribal priests had been replaced by the new line of priests appointed by the kings to the Temple. Ancient sanctuaries, such as Bethel, Shiloh, Shechem and Hebron, were overshadowed by Jerusalem.

The split between the kingdoms was sealed when the northern king, Jeroboam, declared that two of the old sanctuaries, Dan and Bethel, were now the official royal shrines of the northern kingdom. A golden bull was erected in each of them, and while this was a traditional symbol for the Hebrew God, Yahweh, it could easily be seen as a representation of the Canaanite god, Baal. The southern Hebrews denounced the northerners for supporting the Canaanite religion. There is evidence of the truth of this charge in the Bible's accounts of the struggle of such prophets as Elijah and Elisha against the Baal priests in the north. However, the southern Hebrews also encouraged the Canaanite religion up until the end of both kingdoms, and were denounced by such southern prophets as Isaiah and Jeremiah.

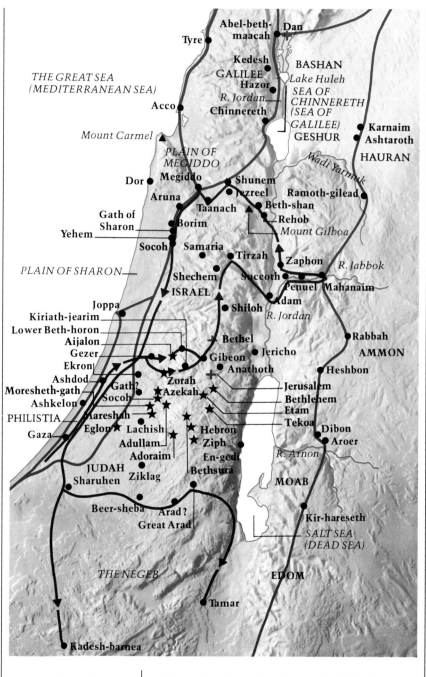

THE GREAT SEA
(MEDITERRANEAN SEA)

Abel-beth-
maacah   Dan

Tyre

Kedesh
GALILEE   BASHAN
Hazor   *Lake Huleh*
          SEA OF
R. Jordan   CHINNERETH
Acco   (SEA OF
Chinnereth   GALILEE)
            GESHUR   Karnaim
Mount Carmel   Ashtaroth
PLAIN OF   HAURAN
MEGIDDO   *Wadi Yarmuk*

Dor   Megiddo
      Shunem
Aruna   Jezreel   Ramoth-gilead
Taanach   Beth-shan
Gath of   Borim   Rehob
Sharon   *Mount Gilboa*
Yehem
Socoh   Samaria   Zaphon
                R. Jabbok
PLAIN OF SHARON   Tirzah
      Shechem   Succoth
      ISRAEL   Penuel Mahanaim
            Adam
Joppa   Shiloh   *R. Jordan*
Kiriath-jearim
Lower Beth-horon
Aijalon   Bethel
Gezer   Gibeon   Jericho   Rabbah
Ekron   Anathoth   AMMON
Ashdod   Heshbon
Moresheth-gath   Zorah
Ashkelon   Gath? Azekah   Jerusalem
PHILISTIA   Socoh   Bethlehem
   Mareshah   Etam
Gaza   Eglon   Lachish   Tekoa
      Adullam   Hebron   Dibon
         Ziph   Aroer
      Adoraim
JUDAH   En-gedi   *R. Arnon*
Sharuhen   Ziklag   Bethsura
         MOAB

Beer-sheba   Arad?
Great Arad   Kir-hareseth
         *SALT SEA
         (DEAD SEA)*

THE NEGEB   EDOM

Tamar

Kadesh-barnea

LEFT *Shortly after
Solomon's death, the
Egyptians, under
Sheshonk I, re-established
control of Palestine, taking
command of Jerusalem
and the trade routes.
Rehoboam, Solomon's
successor, quickly
alienated the northern
tribes by establishing his
power base in the south.
The northern kingdom,
which existed only for two
centuries, was by far the
more prosperous and
stronger of the two
kingdoms, but it was
crushed by the Assyrians
in 721 BC and its capital
was destroyed.*

*Sheshank and the
Egyptian
campaign,
c 928 BC*

★ *King Rehoboam
of Judah's
fortresses*

✛ *Royal sanctuaries*

*Major trade
routes*

Egypt had regained control of the Palestinian coastal route to the north and to Mesopotamia, but her supremacy was short-lived. During the eighth century BC Egypt was once more torn by civil war, and the Assyrians of Mesopotamia had begun the great expansion which would soon give them possession of the Middle East from the Persian Gulf to Upper Egypt.

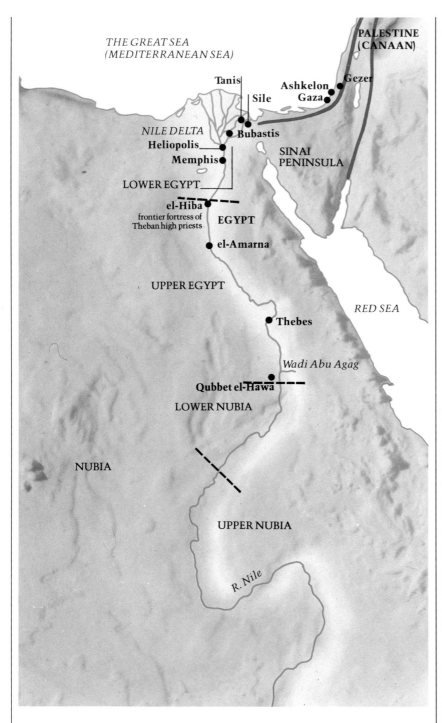

THE GREAT SEA
(MEDITERRANEAN SEA)

PALESTINE
(CANAAN)

Tanis
Sile
Ashkelon
Gaza
Gezer

NILE DELTA
Bubastis
Heliopolis
Memphis

SINAI
PENINSULA

LOWER EGYPT

el-Hiba
frontier fortress of
Theban high priests

EGYPT

el-Amarna

UPPER EGYPT

RED SEA

Thebes

Wadi Abu Agag

Qubbet el-Hawa

LOWER NUBIA

NUBIA

UPPER NUBIA

R. Nile

ABOVE *Such a long, narrow kingdom as Egypt soon split into warring factions if the central government was weak. The Tanis kings controlled the Nile delta area, but were only* *nominal sovereigns of Upper Egypt which was ruled by the Theban priests, who acknowledged the Tanis kings.*

- - - - Frontiers
────── Major trade
routes

The Decline of Egypt

When the Hebrews escaped from Egypt to create a new nation in Palestine, Egypt was breaking into its two natural divisions, Upper and Lower Egypt. The attempted invasions by the 'Sea Peoples' (the Philistines) and the Libyans were stretching Egyptian defences to their limits. The Egyptians were in no position to prevent the Hebrews from penetrating into eastern Palestine, nor to stop the Philistines taking over the western coast.

Two centuries later, during the reigns of the Hebrew Kings David and Solomon, Lower Egypt was ruled from Tanis in the Nile delta where the coastal road leaves Egypt for Palestine and Mesopotamia. Theoretically, Upper Egypt was also ruled from Tanis, but

the priests of Thebes, the southern Egyptian capital, acted as an independent kingdom under the leadership of their hereditary high priest. The Tanis kings could only enforce their authority as far as the frontier fortress of el-Hiba, 60 miles (100 km) up the River Nile from Memphis.

Solomon's Temple Stripped

Egypt revived for a while under the first king of the next dynasty, a Libyan called Sheshonk, who was determined to regain full control of Palestine with its vital international routes. It was he who invaded the southern Hebrew kingdom of Judah and stripped the royal palace and the Temple of their treasures before returning to Egypt again.

BELOW *A fallen statue – a vivid symbol of a fallen dynasty in a divided Egypt.*

For a while Sheshonk managed to impose his rule over both parts of Egypt, but the unity was not to last. On his death, the country disintegrated once more into overlapping dynasties and areas ruled by independent cities with their own kings. The central Egyptian government could no longer assert any effective power. Soon, in the eighth century BC, the Assyrians would be rolling ruthlessly across the near east from Mesopotamia, through Palestine and into Egypt itself.

Egyptian royal tombs from this turbulent period have been excavated within the Temple area at Tanis, the capital of Lower Egypt. They reveal brick walls 30 feet (10 m) high and 45 feet (15 m) thick enclosing an area 500 yards (430 m) long by 400 yards (370 m) wide. Clearly, the uncertain times demanded that the temples should be turned into massive fortresses, where the state treasuries and the burial shrines of Egypt's divine kings could be safely guarded.

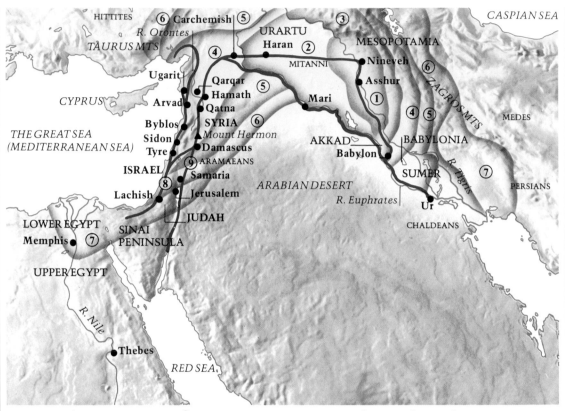

① *Nucleus of the Assyrian Empire*

② *Expansion in 14th century BC*

③ *Expansion in 13th century BC*

④ *Expansion in 9th century BC*

⑤ *Expansion during the reign of Tiglath-pileser III (745–727 BC)*

⑥ *Expansion during reigns of Sargon II (721–705 BC) and Sennacherib (704–681 BC)*

⑦ *Expansion during reigns of Esarhaddon (680–669 BC) and Ashurbanipal (668–630 BC)*

— *Major trade routes*

⑧ *The Way of the Sea*

⑨ *The King's Highway*

Anvil of the Powers

In the tenth century BC, not long after the death of the Hebrew King Solomon, a succession of Assyrian kings in Mesopotamia broke the power of their eastern enemies, subjugated the Babylonians to the south, and set about expanding Assyrian rule westwards towards the Great Sea. For a while the Assyrians were held in check by a coalition of 11 kings from Syria, Lebanon and Palestine, including the Hebrews, who defeated the Assyrians at the Battle of Qarqar on the River Orontes in 854 BC.

Soon, however, Assyrian patrols were probing into Palestine down the coastal road towards Egypt, and along the King's Highway on the eastern edge of the Jordan Valley. The Assyrians were not ready to occupy the region but the Palestinian kingdoms began to feel the pressure of Assyrian power. King Jehu of Israel, the northern Hebrew kingdom, bought off the Assyrian King Shalmaneser III with ingots of silver and gold, and vessels made of gold, but gained only a temporary respite for his people.

Assyria's Advance

New impetus was given to the Assyrian expansion by the most dynamic of its kings, Tiglath-pileser III, who crushed all opposition as his armies drove down through Palestine. Under Tiglath-pileser III and his successors, Assyria became the first power to create an empire stretching through the whole of the 'fertile crescent', from the Persian Gulf to Lower Egypt, with the international routes through Palestine as its main arteries. The two Hebrew kingdoms found themselves on opposite sides of the vital Assyrian lines of communication, and could not hope to retain their independence.

Tiglath-pileser III incorporated northern Palestine, including the Hebrew kingdom of Israel, into an Assyrian province, and exacted tribute from Judah, the southern Hebrew kingdom. Despite the fierce opposition of the prophet Isaiah, King Ahaz of Judah turned the small kingdom of Judah into an outpost of Assyrian power, and converted Solomon's great Temple into a shrine of the Assyrian religion to prove his loyalty to his new

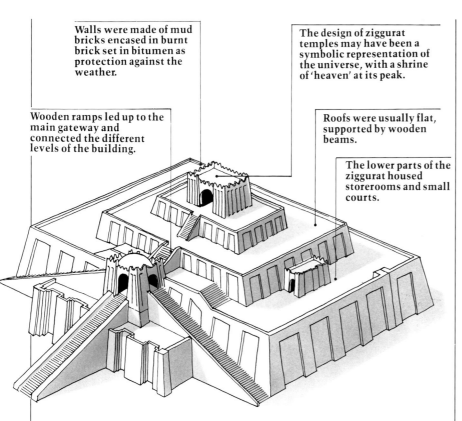

Walls were made of mud bricks encased in burnt brick set in bitumen as protection against the weather.

Wooden ramps led up to the main gateway and connected the different levels of the building.

The design of ziggurat temples may have been a symbolic representation of the universe, with a shrine of 'heaven' at its peak.

Roofs were usually flat, supported by wooden beams.

The lower parts of the ziggurat housed storerooms and small courts.

Assyria finally defeated the Egyptians early in the seventh century BC. However they did not manage to maintain effective control over their Egyptian possessions, for the empire was far too extended even for Assyrian armies. It collapsed quickly under the pressure of Scythian incursions from the east, and a rebellion by the Babylonians who captured the Assyrian capital, Nineveh in 612 BC and took over the empire.

The Assyrians worshiped a complex pantheon of 600 planetary and stellar deities, and 300 gods of the land of the dead. They also had a creation myth which included a tradition of a universal flood similar to the opening chapters of Genesis. The most dramatic remains of their religion are the great temple towers, the ziggurats, which have been unearthed from the upper reaches of the River Euphrates to the Persian Gulf.

The Babylonians

After the Babylonians had destroyed the Assyrian capital of Nineveh, they went on to defeat their other potential rival for power,

masters. It is hardly surprising that Isaiah's messianic prophecies date from this time: the Hebrews were desperately in need of a messiah who would bring them back to the covenant with God.

Deportations

The Assyrians completed the destruction of the northern Hebrew kingdom, Israel, and its capital Samaria, in 721 BC after a brief rebellion. The Hebrew population was deported (disappearing from history) and replaced with settlers from other parts of the empire. Twenty years later, rebellions erupted throughout the empire and the Palestinian states appealed to Egypt for help. An Egyptian army did march north but it was easily defeated by the Assyrians. King Hezekiah of Judah had seized the opportunity to reform his people's religion with the help of Isaiah, but the Assyrians besieged Jerusalem and accepted Hezekiah's submission after he had paid a crippling sum in tribute. There was to be no respite.

ABOVE *Ziggurats were built by the Mesopotamians to worship their astrology gods. Notable examples of ruined ziggurats are those at Ur and Khorsbad in Mesopotamia. These towering temples are an example of the energy and imagination of this ancient people, and a vivid expression of their religious beliefs.*

RIGHT *Like the Assyrians, the Babylonians worshipped a multitude of deities, some of which entered Hebrew folk traditions. This night demon is the model for 'Lilith' in the Hebrew stories.*

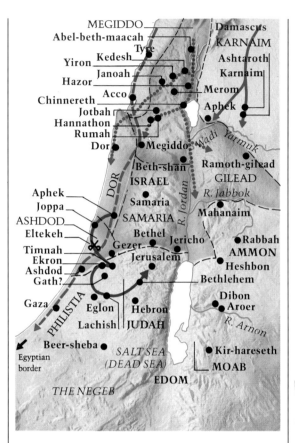

MEGIDDO
Abel-beth-maacah
Yiron   Kedesh   Tyre
Janoah
Hazor
Chinnereth   Acco
Jotbah
Hannathon
Rumah
Dor   Megiddo

Damascus
KARNAIM
Ashtaroth
Karnaim
Merom
Aphek

Wadi Yarmuk

DOR
Beth-shan   Ramoth-gilead
ISRAEL   GILEAD
R. Jabbok

Aphek
Joppa   Samaria
ASHDOD   SAMARIA   Mahanaim
Eltekeh   Bethel
Gezer   Jericho   Rabbah
Timnah   Jerusalem   AMMON
Ekron   Heshbon
Ashdod
Gath?   Bethlehem

R. Jordan

Dibon
Aroer
Gaza   Eglon   Hebron   R. Arnon
Lachish   JUDAH

Beer-sheba   SALT SEA   Kir-hareseth
Egyptian   (DEAD SEA)   MOAB
border
EDOM
THE NEGEB

PHILISTIA

LEFT *The Hebrew kingdoms were subject to several military incursions when the Assyrians were led by Tiglath-pileser III. After advancing into Egypt along the coast, the Assyrians captured Damascus from the Syrians in 732 BC and exacted tribute. In 701 BC an operation was mounted against Judah. When Samaria was destroyed in 721 BC, Judah survived by becoming a puppet kingdom of the Assyrians. Hezekiah, King of Judah, was forced to pay tribute to the Assyrians, despite the support of Egypt.*

--- *Route of Tiglath-pileser III in 734 BC*

••••••• *Route of Tiglath-pileser III in 733 BC*

—— *Route of Tiglath-pileser III in 732 BC*

Assyrian provinces

Expansion of Shalmaneser V and Sargon II, and provinces

—— *Route of Sennacherib's in 701 BC*

✂ *Defeat of Egyptian army, 701 BC*

the Egyptians, at Carchemish, on the borders of modern-day Syria and Turkey, and so gained control of Palestine. At first the Babylonians did little to trouble the only remaining Hebrew kingdom, Judah, and they allowed King Jehoiakim to continue ruling from his capital, Jerusalem. The Hebrews, however, once more appealed to the Egyptians to free them from foreign rule, and when the Babylonians heard of this they attacked Jerusalem and captured it after a three month siege.

Jerusalem Destroyed

The Hebrew king and his leading officials were all deported to Babylon, where they were allowed to live at Babylonian expense in some comfort. However, the new Hebrew government in Jerusalem continued intrigues with Egypt, despite the opposition of the prophet Jeremiah, and in 589 BC the Babylonians again attacked Jerusalem. This time the siege lasted nearly three years. Despite a

brief respite when an Egyptian army tried to relieve the city, the Babylonians finally destroyed it and deported king and people to Babylonia where the Hebrew monarchy ended. Palestine was lost to the Hebrews for 1the 48 years of their exile, until the Babylonians in their turn were overthrown by the Persians in 539 BC.

As a result of the exile, the city of Babylon became a symbol of oppression and corruption, instantly recognizable in the Bible by both Jews and Christians as typical of any powerful enemy. Situated on the river Euphrates near the south-eastern limits of Mesopotamia, the city and its people were far more tolerant than the Assyrians. It is significant that the exiled Hebrews in Babylonia retained their national identity and were able to use the exile period to give new meaning and vitality to their religion. The Babylonians' religion was a form of the beliefs predominant in Mesopotamia, with temple towers, a vast pantheon of gods, divination to discover the will of the gods and belief in a multitude of demons.

The Protest Movement

As the two Hebrew kingdoms came to terms with the new political and international scene after the death of King Solomon, the northern kingdom of Israel grew ever more prosperous from the great trading routes, by contrast with its southern neighbour, Judah. The weak control Egypt exercised over Palestine had little effect on the Hebrew kingdoms.

With prosperity came deep social stratification, stark inequality and injustice. The very shape of the towns changed as the wealthy Hebrews enlarged their houses at the expense of their poorer neighbours and forced them to crowd into the less attractive parts. Many people sold their land to meet their debts and slid inexorably into slavery. There was no redress for the poor in the corrupt courts of law.

The traditional Hebrew religion of the covenant insisted that the poor must be protected, and valued justice about all political virtues protected by divine law. This traditional religion still received recognition—with some adaptations to the newly acquired agricultural skills—in the ancient sanctuaries

New Terror

ABOVE *Vines growing near Lachish. In their teaching, the prophets promised prosperity, symbolized by vines, for obedience to God, and the catastrophes like the Assyrian destruction of Lachish for disobedience.*

of Palestine, such as Beer-sheba, Hebron, Bethel, Shiloh, Shechem, Dan, Mount Carmel, Mount Ebal, Mount Gerizim and Mount Hermon. In addition, there was the new Temple built by King Solomon in Jerusalem to house the main symbol of the Hebrew religion and its sacred law: the Ark of the Covenant. However, many Hebrews had adopted the native Canaanite religion of Baal, with its law of might, its worship of the fertility gods and goddesses, human sacrifice and sacred prostitution at the 'high places'. In such a religion the poor and weak had no rights.

Fearless Teachers

In this situation a new group of religious leaders emerged, the prophets. They were fearless popular teachers, independent of the royal courts and official sanctuaries. They were prepared to denounce kings, priests and judges as they stole their subjects' lands,

gave official recognition to the Baal religion, and maintained their power ruthlessly by torture and murder. Often, the prophets paid for their courage with their lives.

The first of the prophets to leave a book of his teachings was Amos, a shepherd from the south who denounced the northern kings and their administration at the royal sanctuary of Bethel. A little later, Hosea continued Amos's work, and taught that the Hebrew God of the covenant, Yahweh, was the real source of his people's prosperity, not the Canaanite fertility gods. Hosea opened the way for a new, less legalistic understanding of the covenant with God by teaching that he is a forgiving God, whose tender, steadfast love will always save the Hebrews.

Israel Destroyed

The most famous prophet at this time was Isaiah, who taught in the southern Hebrew kingdom, Judah, at the time when the

Assyrians began their drive southwards into Palestine to secure their frontiers with Egypt. King Ahaz of Jerusalem saw that the Assyrians were too powerful to be stopped, so he seized the opportunity to become an ally of the Assyrians and adopted the Assyrian religion to prove his loyalty. Despite Isaiah's protests, Ahaz replaced the traditional Hebrew religion with Assyrian worship in the Temple in Jerusalem and made Judah an Assyrian base. Isaiah tried to stop Ahaz with the famous 'Immanuel' warning (Isa 7:14), and when he was ignored went on to teach that God would save his people with a faithful and just king, a 'messiah'.

Backed by Judah, the Assyrians destroyed the northern Hebrew kingdom, Israel, in 721 BC, deported its people and replaced them with groups from other parts of the Assyrian empire. The capital of Israel was Samaria, and in these groups of incomers who settled in Samaria and its district we can see the first beginnings of the 'Samaritans' so hated by

ABOVE *Jews with a scroll. The scrolls of the sacred Hebrew writings included the teachings of the prophets, who were often more influential through their writings, after their death, than their preaching during their lifetime.*

the southern Jews in New Testament times. Despite a brief rebellion by King Ahaz's successor, Hezekiah, which the Assyrians suppressed, Judah and Jerusalem survived intact, but only as a firm ally of the Assyrians.

Caught in the age-old dilemma of small nations trying to survive when the great international powers fought each other across small nations' lands, each of the Hebrew kingdoms was eventually destroyed. Israel, the northern kingdom was wiped out by the Assyrians early in their occupation of Palestine and its people were deported never to return. (Since then, various people have claimed to be 'the lost tribes of Israel', including British and American groups.) Judah, the southern kingdom, managed to survive for the remaining hundred years of the Assyrians, only to fall to the Babylonians. The people of Judah eventually emerged again after nearly 50 years of exile in Babylonia, and rebuilt their nation to become the 'Jews', but it was a miraculous survival.

Preserving the Traditions

Throughout the long years of turmoil, and political and religious compromise, a succession of great prophets fought to keep the Hebrew people faithful to the God of the covenant: Elijah, Elisha, Amos, Hosea, Isaiah, Micah, Jeremiah, Habbakuk and Ezekiel, to name but some of them. Although they failed to influence political events, they did help keep alive the main features of the Hebrew religion and in particular the vital importance of justice and righteousness as expressions of God's rule and love.

Other forces also helped preserve the nation's religious traditions. Despite its use by 'foreign' priests and religions, the great Temple in Jerusalem remained a visible reminder of the escape from Egypt and the covenant while the Ark of the Covenant was enshrined in its innermost sanctuary. The psalms preserved the essential beliefs of the

ABOVE *The Western Wall of the Temple in Jerusalem. Even now, the foundations of the great platform on which the Temple stood are the focus for keeping alive Hebrew traditions. In his reforms, King Josiah made the Temple the only national centre for the Hebrew religion.*

Hebrew faith as popular songs, as also did the collections of folk wisdom found in such books of the Bible as Proverbs and Ecclesiasticus.

Above all, the central principles of Hebrew law were still preserved, no matter how corrupt the courts might have become as they administered it, for there was no real distinction between the religious and the secular in everyday life. All actions and transactions came within the sphere of religion, as the Bible shows, and this could still be the traditional Hebrew religion if only it had the support of the nation's leaders.

The Great Reform

Hebrew religious insights were never fixed and unchangeable, but developed steadily as the people coped with life, first under Assyrian occupation, then under the Babylonians—including the long years of exile—and on into the Persian period. Towards the end of the seventh century BC the Hebrews of Judah suddenly found themselves free from foreign occupation for a brief 15 years. They seized the opportunity to make sweeping reforms and to dedicate the nation to God again.

The long reign of Manasseh of Judah (687–642 BC) was a disaster for his people with religious chaos and complete subjection to the Assyrians. Manasseh practised human sacrifice at the terrible Molech shrine just outside Jerusalem. The Temple itself was made a centre for the Assyrian astrological worship of the plants and stars, and the sacred prostitution of the Canaanite fertility religion. The example of Jerusalem was imitated throughout the country and no one dared to protest.

Then quite suddenly the overstretched Assyrian empire disintegrated. Egypt broke away, and at the other end of the empire in Mesopotamia the Babylonians rebelled. Hordes of Scythians swept into Mesopotamia from the eastern mountain ranges and forced the Assyrians to withdraw their troops from Palestine to protect their homelands. They never returned.

Enforcing the Law

King Josiah of Judah (640–609 BC), supported by the young prophet Jeremiah, seized the chance to repair the Temple in Jerusalem as the Assyrians withdrew, and to establish the supremacy of the traditional Hebrew religion again. Soon after the work on the Temple had begun, masons working on the walls found a large scroll hidden in the stonework. It proved to be the full codification of Hebrew law, and occupies most of the biblical Book of Deuteronomy. It showed how Hebrew law applies the central insights of the covenant with God to every detail of daily life, and gives clear, practical rules for the whole range of religious and secular activities in a society, from worship to town planning.

Josiah set out to enforce the laws of Deuteronomy in his kingdom and in the former kingdom of Israel. He removed all traces of the Baal cult and the Assyrian religion from the Temple and from the 'high

places', and destroyed the shrine of Molech outside the southern walls of Jerusalem where children were sacrificed. From now onwards (and still so today), the Temple in Jerusalem was to be the only place in the world where the main sacrificial rites of the Hebrew religion could be performed legally, under the strict supervision of the official priests. It was this regulation which made Jerusalem the centre of pilgrimage for Jews throughout the world.

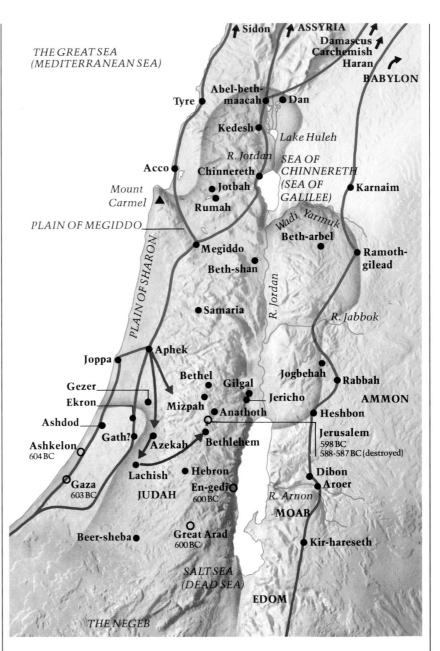

ABOVE *The ruins in the older part of Jerusalem have been excavated and confirm the deliberate destruction of the city in 587 BC.*

LEFT *The Babylonians turned their attention to the 'fertile crescent' after vanquishing the Assyrians in Mesopotamia. At the same time King Josiah was introducing his religious reforms, destroying the shrines of foreign religions, and giving new life to the old Hebrew laws of the covenant. Under Nebuchadnezzar the invaders were a much stronger and more unified force; they captured important towns including Jerusalem which they took in 598 BC and then destroyed almost 10 years later.*

The King's Mistake

Carried away by the success of his reform, King Josiah of Judah thought that God would keep his kingdom safe from foreign interference. It was a fatal mistake. The Egyptian King Necho II marched an army through Palestine in 609 BC to support the Assyrians in their final struggle against the Babylonians, in an attempt to maintain the balance of power in the Near and Middle East. The Egyptians failed and Babylonia rose to supremacy, but it ended the brief spell of freedom for the Hebrews, as Josiah tried to oppose the passage of the Egyptian army and was killed at the battle of Megiddo.

Josiah's death in 609 BC was the beginning of the end for the Hebrew kingdom of Judah, and for the line of kings directly descended from King David. Egypt took control of Palestine again, but only for four years until the Babylonians destroyed the last Assyrian army in 605 BC. Later that same year the Babylonian king, Nebuchadnezzar, drove southwards through Palestine to attack the Egyptians. The Babylonians were repulsed by the Egyptians with heavy losses, but Nebuchadnezzar kept hold of Palestine and King Jehoiakim of Judah submitted his kingdom and his people to him.

The First Exiles

After the long years of Assyrian domination, the Hebrews of Judah expected the Babylonians to be as ruthless as the power they had overthrown. Both the king and people hoped that Egypt would regain control of Palestine so that they could benefit from the milder rule of Egypt. King Jehoiakim stopped the tribute payments to the Babylonians,

43

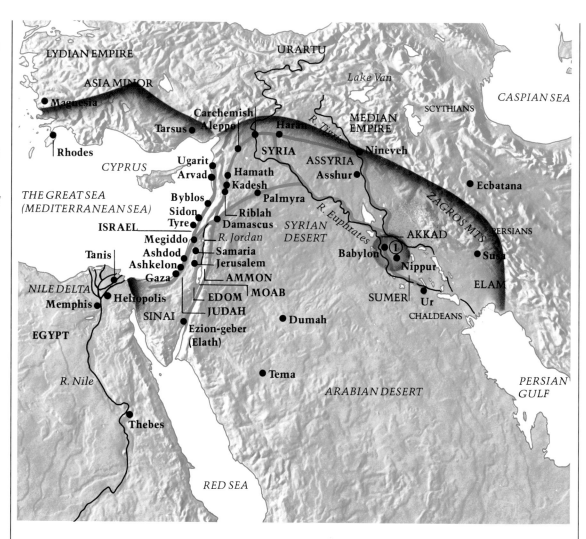

Limits of Babylonian Empire

Major trade routes

① Probable site of exile

called for Egyptian help and trusted to the strength of Jerusalem and an Egyptian victory over the Babylonians.

He died before he could learn how mistaken he was, for it was his son, Jehoiachin, who surrendered Jerusalem to the Babylonians after a siege of three months in 598 BC. The Babylonians were remarkably lenient to the Hebrew people and their leaders, perhaps because they had been spared taking Jerusalem by assault. King Jehoiachin and his court were taken to a comfortable captivity in Babylon from which they expected to be released at any moment, despite the repeated warnings of such prophets as Jeremiah and Ezekiel. Although Jerusalem was not yet destroyed, this was the beginning of the long exile of the Hebrew people in Babylonia, which was to have such deep effects on the

Hebrews' understanding of their religion and on the Bible. Through his visions of God manifesting himself in Babylonia, Ezekiel realized that God had deserted Jerusalem and the Temple and was now with the exiles in Babylonia, but Ezekiel could not convince the exiles or the Hebrews of Jerusalem. They would not be convinced until Jerusalem was destroyed.

Destruction of Jerusalem

The new Hebrew king in Jerusalem, Zedekiah, foolishly thought that Babylonian leniency was a sign of weakness and called again for Egyptian help to support a Hebrew rebellion. This time Jerusalem resisted the inevitable

LEFT *The Jews' experiences in the wilderness or in exile at all stages of their history have helped to define their national identity and bring them closer to God. Jesus himself went into the wilderness to be alone with God.*

Babylonian siege for nearly three years and when it was finally taken in 587 BC the Babylonians destroyed it. Zedekiah's two sons were executed before him and Zedekiah taken in chains to Babylon together with the bulk of the people. The kingdom of Judah was finished, all its cities in ruins and only the poorest of its people, left scattered, remained. Although the Hebrews would retain their identity in Babylonia, and would never forget the glory of David and Solomon when they were the undisputed masters of Palestine, it would be 48 years before the Hebrew exiles could return to build their capital and their nation.

The Exile in Babylonia

The long exile in Babylonia from 587 to 539 BC deprived the Hebrews of most of the visible symbols of their covenant religion. The Temple of Jerusalem and the Ark of the Covenant were destroyed, and this had been the only place where they could offer the sacrifices of animals and crops central to their worship. The long line of Davidic kings ends with the Babylonian exile and the destruction of David's capital, Jerusalem. These kings had been the visible guardians of God's covenant, no matter how they had failed. However, the most powerful covenant symbol of all was Palestine itself, the Holy Land, promised to them by God, and the exiles were separated from it apparently indefinitely.

The exiles had in fact taken with them other symbols of their religion as powerful as the ones they had lost, had they but known it. These were their historical traditions, which recorded in oral form no less than in writing how God had made himself known to the people's ancestors, in the escape from Egypt, and in the triumphs of David. They also had their legal traditions, formulated as expressions of the covenant, and their memories of the sacred rituals of the Temple of Jerusalem, including the hymns and music they used in their worship and which they could still sing in Babylonia. The Hebrew priests became the guardians of the nation's traditions now that they could no longer preside over the sacrifices. This ensured that the Hebrew

RIGHT *On the River Euphrates, a little way to the south of modern Baghdad stood the ancient city of Babylon. From here the rulers of Babylon controlled the whole of southern Mesopotamia. Babylon was defended by a double wall with eight gates, and straddled the river Euphrates. The old city was connected to its new extensions by two bridges. The city was divided into sections by great avenues and there was also a network of canals. The city was built of hard baked mud bricks with imaginative relief sculptures reflecting the impressive architecture. Babylon was the centre of the empire in the second millenium BC. It later fell into decline and became an Assyrian province. However, the Babylonians rebelled in 626 BC and eventually overthrew the Assyrian Empire in 612 BC.*

ABOVE *The main entrance into Babylon was through the Ishtar Gate. The gate itself was covered with blue enamelled brick reliefs of bulls and dragons. The adjacent buildings had friezes of lions on their walls. In the New Year festival, a statue of Marduk, the chief god of Babylon, was carried in procession along an avenue and through the Ishtar Gate. The great avenue stretched right across the city and was paved with pink marble and limestone.*